MINNESOTA
A PHOTOGRAPHIC CELEBRATION

photography by
Richard Hamilton Smith

Compiled by the staff of
American Geographic Publishing

ISBN 0-938314-76-9

Photography © 1989 Richard Hamilton Smith.

© 1989 American Geographic Publishing
P.O. Box 5630, Helena, MT 59604
(406) 443-2842

William A. Cordingley, Chairman
Rick Graetz, Publisher & CEO
Mark O. Thompson, Director of Publications
Barbara Fifer, Production Manager
Design by Linda Collins

Printed in Korea by Dong-A Printing and Publishing
through Codra Enterprises, Torrance, California

American Geographic Publishing is a corporation for publishing illustrated geographic information and guides. It is not associated with American Geographical Society. It has no commercial or legal relationship to and should not be confused with any other company, society or group using the words geographic or geographical in its name or its publications.

Left: Near the Boundary
Waters Canoe Area,
northeastern Minnesota.
Below: Soybean field near
Welch Village, south of the
Twin Cities.
Facing page: At Stillwater.

Title page: Near Warroad in
northwestern Minnesota.

Front cover: In the Boundary
Waters Canoe Area.

Back cover, top: Aerial view
of the Minnesota Capitol, St.
Paul.
Left: On Burntside Lake.
Right: Cross-country time in
the Twin Cities.

3

Richard Hamilton Smith lives in St. Paul,
Minnesota and travels the world photograph-
ing for corporate, advertising and editorial
clients. His work has appeared in numerous
national periodicals and has received awards
from Communication Arts, Art Direction, Print
and Photo-Design magazines and the Art
Directors/Copywriters Club.

5

Above: *Rice Park and Ordway Music Theater, St. Paul.*
Top: *The Equinox Wall in Blue Mound State Park aligns with the rising sun on the equinox. But who built it?*
Facing page: *A maple forest in central Minnesota.*

Above: *Tractor parade at the Butterfield Antique Steam & Gas Engine Festival.*
Left: *Aerial view of the mixed forest on the north shore of Lake Superior.*

Above: *Harvest and moon on the Estram farm near Cannon Falls.*
Facing page: *Ice ridge on Lake Lida in the Pelican Rapids area.*

Above: *Christmas decorations in downtown Minneapolis.*
Facing page: *The Kodunce River Gorge on the north shore of Lake Superior.*

Above: Oceangoing
freighters approaching the
Duluth harbor.
Right: On the north shore
near Grand Marie.
Facing page: Loose-strife
growing in the Minnesota
River Valley east of St.
Paul.

Above: High Falls, the Pigeon River, viewed over an abandoned logging chute.
Right: Cornfield and cirrus clouds near Rochester.

This is what it looks like where I grew up :)

Above: *Contrasting textures in Blue Mound State Park.*
Facing page: *Runners in the Twin Cities Marathon enter Minneapolis' lakes area; Minneapolis skyline in the background.*

Above: White-tailed deer.
Right: Southeastern Minnesota.

Above: Lutsen Lodge restaurant on the north shore of Lake Superior.
Right: A ship hand directing a moving ship.
Facing page: Near Chisholm in the Iron Range, reclaimed strip-mining pits fill with water.

Above: *Aerial view of fog in the pine forest of the Minnesota-Wisconsin border area.*
Right: *Northland Camp resort on Burntside Lake near Ely.*

Above: The twin spires of St. Paul's Assumption Church contrast with the World Trade Tower.
Right: Near Farmington.
Facing page: The St. Louis River, Jay Cooke State Park.

I rode a bus everyday like this ☺

Above: Study in—almost—black and white, southwestern Minnesota.
Right: Near Luverne.

Above: *A corner of the Minnesota Capitol and the dome of the St. Paul Cathedral.*
Right: *Lupines.*
Facing page: *Grain elevator near Rosemont.*

Overleaf: *On the north shore of Lake Superior near Hovland.*

29

One of our favorite things to do in MN – canoeing. :)

Above: *Jeanne Estrera working the corn harvest on the Estram farm near Cannon Falls.*
Top: *On Blue Lake near Park Rapid.*
Facing page: *Boundary Waters Canoe Area.*

Above: *The Taste of Minnesota celebration, St. Paul.*
Facing page: *Du Nord Island in Burntside Lake, YMCA Camp Du Nord near Ely.*

Above: *Sumac branches frame a farm in the mist.*
Right: *Tugboat and barges on the Mississippi at St. Paul.*

Above: Snow-lined oaks in Como Park, St. Paul.
Top: Talking futures.
Facing page: Rural Fletcher is only a few miles northwest of Minneapolis.

Above: *Meeting a bull moose on Devil Track Lake, northeastern Minnesota.*
Left: *Lake Calhoun, Minneapolis.*

Above: The Red River Valley between Kennedy and Humboldt.
Right: Lake Minnetonka regatta.
Facing page: Ice fishing on the Mississippi near Red Wing.

43

Above: *St. Paul Cathedral reflection.*
Right: *Near La Crescent on the Mississippi.*

Overleaf: *Minneapolis' Nicollet Mall.*

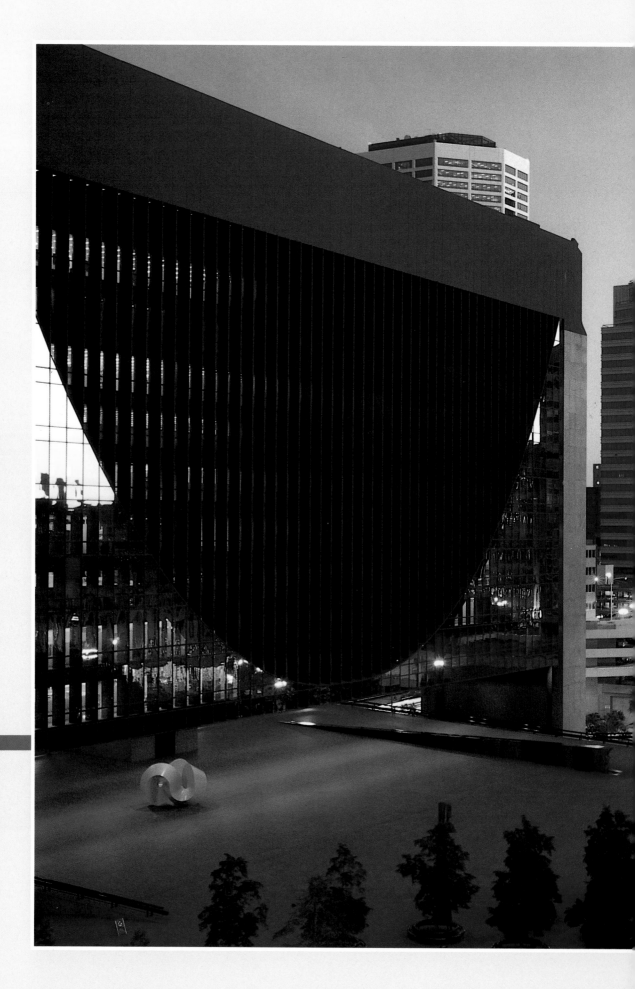

49

Above: *Boise-Cascade mill, International Falls.*
Top: *On the St. Croix River near Stillwater.*
Facing page: *Near Olivia in western Minnesota.*

Above: Birch trees in a snowfall north of Duluth.
Left: South of Hastings, an abandoned farm.

Above: *Old cedar in Whitewater State Park.*
Facing page: *The Mississippi at St. Paul.*

Above: *Planting into twilight near Rochester.*
Right: *The swirling St. Louis River in Jay Cooke State Park.*

Above: *Near International Falls.*
Top: *Twin Cities skylines: St. Paul in the foreground, Minneapolis beyond.*
Facing page: *On the north shore of Lake Superior.*
Overleaf: *Southeastern Minnesota.*

58

Above: Loon.
Right: Above the St. Croix River near Taylors Falls.

Above: *Phalen Park, St. Paul.*
Facing page: *Fenske Lake near Ely, on the Echo Trail.*

Above: *East St. Paul railyard.*
Facing page, top: *Redwood Falls.*
Bottom: *Celebrating St. Paul's Winter Carnival near Como Park.*

Ian's favorite statues!

Above: The Mississippi River near Zumbro, southeastern Minnesota.
Left: The golden quadriga atop the Minnesota Capitol.

Above: *Lake Nokomis, Minneapolis.*
Facing page: *Near Hallock and the North Dakota border.*

Above: *In the Kodunce River Gorge.*
Right: *The Port of Duluth.*

Above: *St. Paul Winter Carnival ice sculptures in Rice Park, with the Ordway Music Theater in the background.*
Right: *East of Mankato.*
Facing page: *Three kinds of highways at St. Paul.*

73

Above: At the Lake Calhoun Aquatennial, Minneapolis.
Left: Lac qui Parle, southwestern Minnesota.

Above: The old Hovland Hotel on the north shore of Lake Superior.
Left: Aerial view of islands in Boundary Waters Canoe Area.
Facing page: Late-summer lupine near Pipestone.

Overleaf: Bogus Lake, far northern Minnesota.

John's grand-
parents live
at Dora Lake
in northern
MN - it looks
a lot like this.
We love it up
there - it's so
peaceful, clean,
and unpopulated.
We hope to
own a place
up there someday.
☺

Above: Marshland in the Minnesota River Valley.
Right: Steaming past the Port of Duluth lighthouse.
Facing page: High Falls on the Pigeon River at the Ontario-Minnesota border.

Above: *A fisheye view of St. Paul and the Mississippi.*
Left: *Taconite mining near Hibbing.*
Facing page: *The Redwood River in Alexander Ramsey Park, Redwood Falls.*

Above: *Pine green contrasts with aspen's spring color.*
Left: *The Mississippi near Winona.*

Above: *Oak tree against the autumn gold of aspens.*
Top: *Phalen Lake in St. Paul.*
Facing page: *Burntside Lake.*

Above: *Lake Calhoun and Minneapolis.*
Left: *Grain-shipping facility, Duluth.*

Above: Chapel Point on Burntside Lake viewed from the Skytrail in the St. Paul YMCA's canoe camp, Camp Widjiwagan. **Left:** Ice climbing along the Manitou River. **Facing page:** Near Ortonville in western Minnesota, a lake of ice covers the ground.

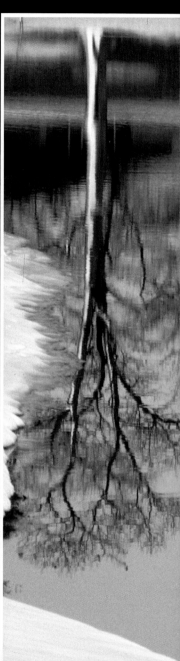

Above: *Stillwater on the St. Croix River.*
Right: *Wintertime reflection.*

Above: *Boise Cascade paper mill at International Falls.*
Left: *In Blue Mound State Park.*
Facing page, top: *Dawn near Rushford.*
Bottom: *Thunderhead boiling up over a farm north of Pine City.*